Contents

Life on Earth 6

Food chains 8

Plants provide food 10

Plants provide shelter 12

Improving the soil 14

Spreading pollen 16

Animals spread seeds 18

Life on an oak tree 20

Life in a pond 22

Carnivorous plants 24

Protecting the environment 26

Glossary 28

Answers to "What's this?" 29

Index 30

Life on Earth

The Earth is home to millions of living things known as organisms. Plants and animals are organisms. They are different from one another but they share some important characteristics.

Kingdoms of life

There are many different organisms in the world around us. To make them easier to study, and to make sure that one organism is not confused with another, scientists have sorted them into different groups. The largest groups, called kingdoms, contain organisms with similar characteristics. Plants and animals are very different from each other so they belong to two different kingdoms.

How are plants and animals different?

Not only do plants and animals look different from each other, but they also behave differently. Most plants are green and have leaves, stems and roots. They are unable to move around. Plants have one very important characteristic: they are able to make food for themselves using sunlight, air and water. Animals cannot make their own food but they are able to find it.

Plants are the only living organisms that can make their own food. This makes them very different from animals.

How are they the same?

Most plants and animals are complicated organisms made up of many cells. They also share other characteristics: they need food to grow; they need water and air; they sense and react to the world around them; they produce young just like themselves; and they eventually die. Animals and plants have lived side by side for many millions of years, and their lives are linked in important ways. This book examines how.

Like all organisms, animals need food to live. A rhinoceros cannot make food for itself but it can move around and use its powerful sense of smell to find it.

Food chains

Plants make food for themselves using sunlight, air and water. They supply food for other living things to eat. This makes them the foundation stone of life on Earth.

Making food

Plants make food for themselves by the process of photosynthesis, which takes place inside their leaves. The leaves use energy from sunlight, water from the soil and a gas, called carbon dioxide, from the air to produce starchy substances called carbohydrates. These give the plants the energy to grow and make new roots, stems, buds and leaves. During photosynthesis, the leaves give off oxygen, a gas all animals need to survive.

Get this!

Some of the world's largest animals feed on plants. The rhinoceros, hippopotamus, gorilla and elephant are all plant eaters, or herbivores.

THE PROCESS OF PHOTOSYNTHESIS

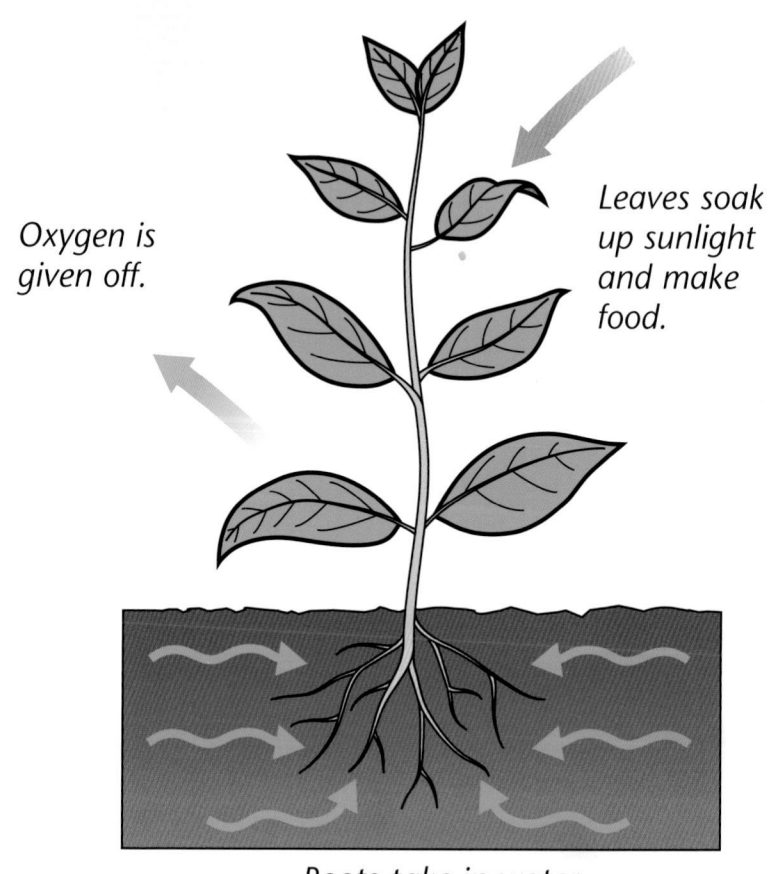

Carbon dioxide enters the leaves from the air.

Oxygen is given off.

Leaves soak up sunlight and make food.

Roots take in water and nutrients.

Links in a chain

Animals cannot make food for themselves; they have to find it. Some animals, such as goats and rabbits, feed directly on plants. They are called herbivores. Other animals, such as eagles and foxes, hunt and feed on herbivores. These meat-eaters are known as carnivores. The plants, herbivores and carnivores are all connected to one another like links in a chain. This is called a food chain.

A plant produces leaves.

A snail feeds on leaves.

A thrush feeds on snails.

Plant foods, such as grass and dandelions, give rabbits and other herbivores the energy to live and grow. In turn, the animals themselves may become food for carnivores.

Producers and consumers

In a food chain, the goodness contained by one organism is passed on to another. At the bottom of a food chain is a plant. Plants produce food for others to eat. They are known as producers. Animals consume food, so they are known as consumers. If plants did not grow, then herbivores would starve. The predators that feed on them would starve, too.

Try this!

Think about the plants and animals that live in your school grounds. Which ones link together to form food chains?

Plants provide food

With their leaves, flowers, fruits and seeds, plants provide animals with food. In some cases, the animals eat so much that plants have adapted to resist them – for example, by growing prickles and thorns.

Plants provide humans with many different foods. Fruit and vegetables are packed with nutrients, and herbs add taste and flavour.

All sorts of food

Plants provide animals with all sorts of food. Mice gnaw on tasty roots; deer strip trees of bark; elephants chew on branches and leaves; aphids suck up sap; fish and other water creatures nibble on leaves, and bees and butterflies suck nectar from flowers. Humans also depend on plants for food. We eat many different plant foods, including nuts, fruit, vegetables, grains and herbs.

Plant defences

If an animal eats too much of a plant, the plant will eventually die. Some plants survive because they have developed special defences to keep animals at bay. For example, the stinging nettle contains a painful poison, the holly tree has prickly leaves, and roses are covered with sharp thorns. However, these defences are not always successful: goats and camels have leathery mouths that can deal with the sharpest thorns.

Get this!

A type of stinging nettle found in Australia grows 15m tall. It has a very unpleasant poison, which causes long-lasting pain.

What's this?

This plant is eaten by zebra, antelope and many other animals. It keeps on growing in spite of this because its shoots lie under the ground.

Feeding adaptations

Food is so important for animals that, over millions of years, some species have adapted or developed in special ways to help them feed more easily. For example, the giraffe's long neck makes it tall enough to eat the leaves at the top of trees. Other animals cannot reach this high, so giraffes always have plenty to eat. Hummingbirds have adapted, too. They beat their wings so swiftly that they can hover in the air and suck up the nectar from many different flowers.

With its long legs and neck, a giraffe can feed on the highest branches of an acacia tree. These are softer, leafier and less thorny than the branches that grow at the base.

11

Plants provide shelter

Plant cover is very important for animals. It hides them from predators or prey, provides a safe place to bring up their young and also protects them from the Sun.

Providing cover

If you have ever seen a squirrel run up a tree or a shrew bolt into the grass, then you will know that plants provide animals with cover. This is very important for prey animals, which are at risk of being hunted. Some animals, such as lizards and moths and butterflies, have even evolved special colouring that helps them to blend in better with plants. This is called camouflage. Camouflage works for predators, too. When a tiger is hunting in long grass, its stripy coat keeps it hidden.

This orange tip butterfly is so well camouflaged, it is easy to mistake it for part of the flower on which it feeds.

Get this!

Crab spiders hunt insects that feed on flowers. The spiders can change their body colour to match their chosen flower.

Try this!

In winter, when trees and hedges are bare, look out for old bird nests. If you find one, take it apart. How many of its materials came from plants?

Concealing young

Plants help animals to hide their young. Butterflies lay their eggs on the underside of leaves where they cannot be seen. Many birds nest in dense reed beds, thick hedgerows, or high up in trees away from predators on the prowl. Plants also provide useful nest-building materials, such as twigs, leaves, seed heads and moss. These help to make strong, warm nests, and also provide the camouflage that makes them hard to see.

Providing shade

In the tropics, the warmest parts of the world, the Sun is very hot. Plants are very important here in providing animals with shade. At midday, birds retreat to bushes and large mammals, such as elephants and lions, rest under the trees. Shade is also important in the temperate zone during the summer months. Plants like pondweed and water lilies shield water creatures, such as fish and frogs, from the Sun's hot rays.

Impala retreat under the shade of trees during the hottest part of the day.

Improving the soil

Plants grow best in moist soil that contains air and nutrients. Animals help to improve the soil. Many species help to fertilise it. Others introduce air to the soil as they burrow underground.

Natural fertiliser

When an animal has eaten a meal, its body digests the food. Any waste material that cannot be used leaves the animal's body in its droppings. These contain minerals and other important nutrients, which fertilise the soil. The droppings may also contain stringy plant fibres, which improve the soil's structure and help it to stay moist. These are important benefits for plants and result in better, healthier growth.

Many gardeners fertilise the soil by mixing in animal droppings, called manure. Manure improves the structure of the soil and adds nutrients that will help future plants to grow.

A cow produces 13,000kg of manure each year. If this manure is spread on the soil, it returns many of the nutrients that were used by the grass the cow has eaten.

Nature's recyclers

Some animals, such as beetles, maggots and grubs, feed on the bodies of dead animals and the rotting remains of plants. As these remains are broken down, the minerals and other nutrients they contain are mixed in with the soil. The animals, known as decomposers, are performing a recycling service. By returning nutrients to the ground, they are helping to fertilise the soil and feed other plants.

How worms help

Earthworms help to improve the soil, too. As a worm tunnels through the ground, it eats soil, leaves and other plant material. This works its way through the worm's body, before passing out as a worm cast – a little pile of fine, very fertile soil. As the worms burrow underground, they turn over and mix the soil, bringing minerals up to the surface and taking plant matter down. Their tiny tunnels loosen the soil and help rainwater to drain away. Without worms, soil would be hard and airless – a difficult place for plants to grow.

Try this!

Some gardeners keep wormeries to make sure they have fertile soil. To make your own wormery, fill a large, empty container with layers of soil and sand, and place old leaves on the top. Dampen the soil with water and add two or three earthworms. Cover the container with a dark cloth and keep it somewhere cool. Every couple of days, feed the worms kitchen leftovers such as vegetable skins, tea bags and egg shells. Check your wormery daily for a couple of weeks. Remember to keep the soil moist. What do you notice?

Spreading pollen

Plants need to reproduce themselves or they will become extinct. Animals help them to do this by spreading pollen from flower to flower. This is known as pollination.

How flowers work

A plant's flowers help it to develop seeds. Each flower has male and female parts. The male parts are small stalks called stamens. The stamens produce a dust called pollen. The female parts include the stigma and the ovary. Although a flower has both male and female parts, it cannot make seeds by itself. The pollen from the stamens of one flower must move to the stigma of another. This process is called pollination.

CROSS-SECTION OF A FLOWER

Stigma
This is a female part of the flower.

Stamens
These are the male parts of the flower. They are covered with pollen.

Ovary
The seeds develop here.

Sepals
These small leaves protect the bud.

What's this?

This tall woodland plant has flower spikes covered in pink-purple bells. Insects crawl deep inside the bells to find the nectar and pollen.

How animals help

Many plants depend on animals to pollinate their flowers. Insects, such as butterflies and bees, are attracted to a flower by its scent and colour, but above all by a sweet juice called nectar. In the tropics, birds and bats also pollinate flowers. As an animal feeds on the nectar, grains of pollen stick to its body. Then, when it feeds at another flower, the pollen from the first flower rubs onto the stigma. The pollen grains fertilise egg cells in the flower, which then develop into seeds.

A hummingbird hovers in mid-air to collect nectar from a flower. The bird is quite unaware that it is collecting pollen, too.

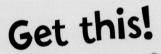

Get this!

Honeybees pollinate more flowers than any other kind of insect. A bee visits up to 10,000 flowers in a single day.

Pollen partners

Most flowers can be pollinated by different kinds of insect. However, some flowers rely on just one species of insect to spread their pollen. These flowers have adapted to make sure that the right insect finds them. For example, bee orchids' flowers look and smell like female bees. Male bees are attracted to the flowers, where they pick up pollen.

The bee orchid has developed an unusual way to attract male bees to pollinate its flowers – its flowers resemble female bees!

Animals spread seeds

Many plants depend on animals to spread their seeds. Unlike plants, animals are not rooted in the ground. They can move seeds from the parent plant to places where they are more likely to survive.

Why seeds spread

Seeds need to grow away from the parent plant. If they do not, the young seedlings will be competing with one another and the parent plant for water, nutrients and sunlight. Moving away gives seeds the best possible chance of growth and survival. Plants use different methods to spread their seed. Some species depend on the wind. Some depend on animals, including humans.

When a hungry squirrel eats a nut, it destroys the seed inside. But squirrels also bury stores of nuts, which may then sprout in the spring.

Animals and fruit

Plants use animals in different ways. Many plants grow their seeds inside a fruit. Some fruits are sweet and juicy, and animals feed on them. The seeds pass through the animal's body, unharmed by digestion, then fall out in the animal's droppings. Other fruits, such as acorns, are hard and dry. Many are eaten by birds and squirrels but others are dropped or buried in the ground and safely sprout in the spring.

It is impossible not to pick up seeds on your clothes and shoes when you are in the woods. The seeds are carried away from the parent plant. Who knows where they will drop and grow?

Hooks and spines

Plants also make use of passing animals. The burdock plant produces seeds covered with tiny hooks and spines. These stick on to an animal's coat as it brushes by. In time, the burdock seeds fall to the ground and, with luck, may grow. Humans help plants in the same way. Whenever you walk through thick undergrowth, you are likely to find that you are carrying seeds – for example, on your jumper, trousers or even in the mud on your boots.

Life on an oak tree

Plants and animals live together in many different kinds of habitat. An oak tree is a plant but it is also a habitat. It is home to many organisms, which depend on it for food and shelter.

The tree gives food

An oak tree is a huge plant with a large root system, a thick trunk, and a wide crown with spreading branches. Every year the tree produces thick leaves, flowers called catkins, and thousands of acorns – all of which provide food for animals. Thousands of animals feed on the tree. Some of them, such as squirrels, grubs and other insects, feed on the tree directly. Others, such as birds, are predators that visit the tree in order to catch their prey. All these animals are dependent on the tree for food.

A mature oak tree is home to a huge variety of creatures. The tree and the animals depend on one another in many different ways.

The tree gives shelter

Oak trees also provide many animals with somewhere to live. Some birds, such as owls, nest in holes in the trunk, while other birds and honey bees build their nests on the oak's huge branches. Many smaller animals, such as earthworms and snails, live among the roots. They help to fertilise and condition the soil. The ground is damp and shady under the tree. This provides good growing conditions for toadstools, mosses and ferns.

When birds such as this blue jay pick up acorns from the oak tree, they help to spread the tree's seeds.

Try this!

Even humans depend on the oak tree. Over the centuries, we have used it for dozens of different things. Research some of these uses.

Dependent on animals

The oak tree is dependent on animals, too. Their feathers, fur, egg cases, droppings and dead bodies all collect on the ground, where beetles and other decomposers break them down. The nutrients they release fertilise the soil. Birds and squirrels help the tree, too. As they collect and carry away its acorns, they help to spread the tree's seeds and produce future generations. The animals and the tree depend on one another. This is known as interdependence.

Get this!

A mature oak tree may be home to 30 kinds of bird and thousands of different insects, including 200 kinds of moth.

Life in a pond

Ponds are home to many different plants and animals – from reeds and rushes to fish and frogs. All these organisms have adapted to the pond and, over many millions of years, have become interdependent.

Plant life

The plants in a pond are very important and provide food, shelter and oxygen for animals. Many plants grow leaves that float on the surface, where they can get light for photosynthesis. This gives the plants the energy to grow, and to produce food for animals. Photosynthesis produces oxygen, which is vital for all the creatures in the pond.

Ponds are important habitats for insects, amphibians and other animals. Plants that grow in and around the pond provide food, cover and shade.

Try this!

Many pond-living organisms are too small for us to see. Collect a few drops of pond water and look at them under a microscope. Can you see anything now?

Animal life

Many animals live in ponds, including fish, frogs, newts, snails and insects. These creatures lay their eggs in the water. The eggs hatch into young called larvae that grow up in the pond. Some of the young are eaten by bigger animals, which are hunted in turn by visiting predators, such as herons and snakes. Animal matter falls into the pond, along with leaves and other vegetation. As these rot, they add nutrients to the water and create a fertile mud that helps plants to grow.

Waterlily leaves provide useful platforms, where frogs can sit and catch flies. The leaves also provide cover from predators.

What's this?

This plant grows in lakes and ponds. It has beautiful white or pink flowers and round leaves that float on the surface of the water.

A POND FOOD CHAIN

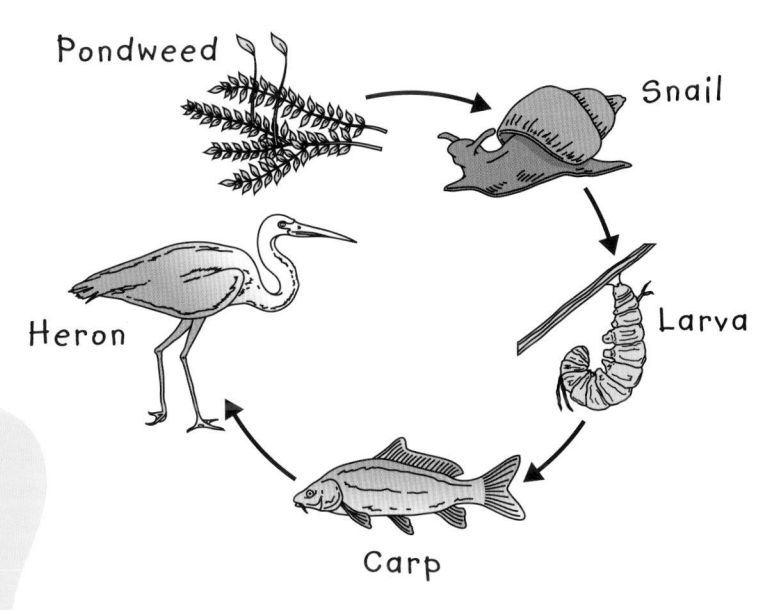

Pondweed — Snail — Larva — Carp — Heron

This is an example of a food chain in a pond. Leaves produce food by the process of photosynthesis and are eaten by pond snails. Dragonfly larvae feed on the snails and carp feed on the larvae. Large birds such as herons feed on the carp.

Carnivorous plants

Plants make food for themselves by photosynthesis. However, a few plant species add meat to their diet to give them extra nutrients. They are known as carnivorous plants.

Why eat meat?

Most plants get all the goodness they need by making their own food and by taking in nutrients from the soil. However, a few plants such as pitcher plants, Venus fly-traps and sundew plants, feed on animals, too. These plants live in poor conditions – for example, on marshland where water washes away nutrients, or on high, rocky ground where the soil is thin. Some species cannot make enough food for themselves because they grow in places with poor sunshine and are starved of light.

Get this!

The inside of the pitcher plant's leaf contains deadly digestive juices. When an insect falls into this acidic mixture, it will be 'eaten' by the plant.

If an insect loses its footing on this pitcher plant, it tumbles into the plant's acid bath, and its body is soon digested.

The Venus fly-trap

A marshland plant called the Venus fly-trap attracts insects to land on its sweet-smelling leaves. When a fly touches sensitive hairs on the leaves, the leaves snap shut, trapping the insect. The leaves then produce a powerful acid that digests the fly's body, changing it to a runny 'soup', which is soaked up by the plant.

A Venus fly-trap has made a successful 'catch'. The nutrients contained in the fly's body will be absorbed by the plant.

The sundew plant's mass of sticky hairs makes an enticing but deadly trap for flies and other small insects.

The sundew plant

The sundew plant grows in bogs and marshes. Its leaves are lined with tiny hairs that are coated with glue. When an insect lands on a leaf, it is trapped by the sticky hairs. The leaf, sensing that it has made a catch, bends over, wraps up the insect and digests its body.

Try this!

Venus fly-traps are often sold at large garden centres. Why not buy one and watch it in action? If you touch its leaves gently with a pencil, they will snap shut. Do not do this too often, though!

Protecting the environment

Protecting our environment is the best way of safeguarding wildlife habitats and the organisms they contain. Adding new plants to schools and gardens is a good place to start.

Habitats around us

Our environment is made up of many different habitats. Some, such as mountains or the seashore, have formed naturally and are very big. Others, such as hedgerows or garden ponds, are smaller and made by people. All these habitats are home to wildlife. The organisms that live in them have built up interdependent relationships, which help them to survive.

- Plants such as teasels can be planted in garden habitats.
- Their seedheads provide tasty seeds that are good for birds.
- In turn the birds help to spread the seeds.

Harmful changes

Our local environment is always changing, often as a result of human action. We cut down trees to build roads and houses; we clear hedges to enlarge a field; we drain and pollute rivers and streams. As a result, habitats that have taken centuries to form can be damaged overnight. But changes can be for the better, too. It is always possible to improve the environment to the benefit of animals and plants.

Where are plants or animals to live in this river in Shanghai, China? The buildings have destroyed their natural habitats and the water is polluted.

Try this!

Plant a pot with brightly coloured flowers. Put a thick layer of gravel in the bottom of the pot, fill it up with potting compost, and then add your plants. Press them down firmly and water well.

Improving the environment

School grounds are part of the local environment and can be important wildlife habitats. Adding new plants, particularly native species, which flower and fruit throughout the year will help to attract animals by providing food. Other ideas for attracting wildlife include planting trees and shrubs to provide cover, piling up rotting vegetation and making a pond.

Glossary

Adapt
The way in which an organism changes in order to survive.

Aphid
A small insect, for example a greenfly, which feeds by sucking the juices from plants.

Camouflage
The colouring on an animal that blends in with the natural surroundings and makes it hard to see.

Carbon dioxide
One of the gases in air. Plants take in carbon dioxide during the process of photosynthesis.

Cells
The tiny parts that join up to make an organism. Cells are sometimes called the 'building blocks' of life.

Decomposer
An animal that feeds on rotting plants and animals, and helps to break them down.

Digestion
The process by which an animal breaks down the food it eats so that it can be used by the body.

Fertilise
To add nutrients to the soil to help plants to grow. Fertilise can also mean when the male and female parts of a flower join together and a seed begins to grow.

Food chain
A chain that shows how food is passed from one organism to another.

Habitat
The place to which an organism is best suited and where it is usually found.

Interdependent
Depending on one another.

Larva
(plural: Larvae) The young stage of an insect or other animal that looks quite different from its parent.

Mineral
A natural substance, often found in the soil, that living things need to survive.

Nectar
A sugary liquid produced by plants to attract insects and other animals.

Nutrient
Any substance that gives an organism energy or helps it to grow.

Oxygen
A gas that is found in air and which all animals need to survive. Plants give out oxygen during photosynthesis.

Photosynthesis
The process by which plants use the energy in sunlight to turn water from the soil and carbon dioxide from the air into starchy substances called carbohydrates.

Pollination

When pollen is carried from the male parts of one flower to the female parts of another.

Predator

An animal that hunts other animals.

Reproduce

To produce offspring. A plant reproduces when it makes new plants.

Species

A group of the same kind of plant. The oak is a species of tree, for example. Holly, yew and beech are also trees, but each one is a different species.

Websites

www.bbc.co.ukschools/revisewise/science/living/06_act.shtml
This interactive website looks at the different parts of plants.

www.naturegrid.org.uk/plant/index.html
Log on to this website to find out more about how people use plants.

www.lanakids.com/plants.html
Find out more about poisonous plants and how to avoid them.

Answers to "What's this"?

Page 11
Grass

Page 16
Foxglove

Page 19
Cherry

Page 23
Water lily

Index

acid 24, 25
acorns 19, 20, 21
air 6, 7, 8, 14, 15, 28, 29
antelope 11
aphids 10, 28

bats 17
bee orchids 17
bees 10, 17
beetles 15, 20
birds 9, 11, 13, 17, 19, 20, 21, 23
bluebells 21
branches 10, 11, 21
buds 8
burdock 19
butterflies 10, 12, 13, 17

camouflage 12, 13, 28
carbohydrates 8, 29
carbon dioxide 8, 28, 29
carnivores 9, 24–25, 28
catkins 20
cells 7, 28
compost 27
consumers 9
cover 12, 22, 27
cows 15

decomposers 15, 20, 28
defences 10
digestion 14, 19, 24, 25, 28
droppings 14, 15, 19, 20

Earth 6, 8
earthworms 15, 21
egg cells 17
eggs 13, 20, 23
elephants 8, 10, 13
energy 8, 22, 28, 29

ferns 21
fertilisation 14, 15, 17, 20, 21, 28
fibres 14
fish 10, 13, 22, 23
flowers 10, 11, 12, 16, 17, 20, 21, 23, 27, 28, 29
food 6, 7, 8, 9, 10–11, 14, 19, 20 21, 22, 23, 24, 27, 28, 29
food chains 9, 23, 28
frogs 13, 22, 23, 24
fruits 10, 19, 27

giraffe 11
goats 9, 10
gorilla 8
grass 12, 15, 29
grubs 15, 21

habitats 20, 22, 26, 27, 28
hedges 13, 26, 27
herbivores 8, 9, 28
hippopotamus 8
holly tree 10, 29
humans 10, 18, 19, 21, 27

insects 12, 16, 17, 21, 22, 23, 25, 28
interdependence 20, 22, 26, 28

kingdoms 6, 7

larvae 23, 28
leaves 6, 8, 9, 10, 11, 13, 15, 20, 21, 22, 23, 25

maggots 15
manure 14, 15
marshland 24, 25
mice 10, 27
minerals 14, 15, 28
moss 13, 21
moths 12, 21
mud 23

nectar 10, 11, 16, 17, 27, 28
nests 13
nutrients 10, 14, 15, 18, 20, 23, 24, 25, 28

organisms 6, 7, 9, 20, 22, 26, 28, 29
oxygen 8, 22, 29

parent plants 18, 19
petals 16
photosynthesis 8, 22, 23, 24, 28, 29
pitcher plants 24
poisons 10
pollen and pollination 16, 17, 29
ponds 22–23, 26, 27
pondweed 13
predators 9, 12, 13, 21, 23, 29

prey 12, 21
producers 9

rabbits 9
reeds 13, 22
reproduction 16, 29
rhinoceros 7, 8
roots 6, 8, 10, 21

sap 10
seashores 26
seeds 10, 13, 16, 17, 18–19, 20, 27, 28
shade 13, 21, 22
shelter 11–12, 13, 20, 21, 22
shoots 12
shrews 11
snails 9, 21, 23
soil 8, 14–15, 20, 21, 24, 28, 29
species 7, 11, 18, 24, 27, 29
spring 18, 19
squirrels 12, 18, 19, 20, 21
stamens 16
stems 6, 8
stigma 16, 17
stinging nettles 10
summer 13
Sun and sunlight 6, 8, 12, 13, 18, 21, 24, 22, 29
sundew plant 24, 25

temperate zone 13
thorns 10, 11
toadstools 21
trees 10, 11, 12, 13, 27, 29
oak trees 20–21, 29
tropics 13, 17
trunks 21
twigs 13

vegetables 10, 24
Venus fly-traps 25

water 6, 7, 8, 10, 13, 15, 18, 22, 24, 26, 27, 29
water lilies 13, 23, 29
wind 18
wings 11
winter 13
worm cast 15
wormeries 15